The Language of Success

Transform Your Life with Effective Communication Skills

Jerome Middleton

loss due to the information herein, either directly or indirectly. Respective authors own all copyrights not held by the publisher. The information herein is offered for informational purposes solely, and is universal as so. The presentation of the information is without contract or any type of guarantee assurance. The trademarks that are used are without any consent, and the publication of the trademark is without permission or backing by the trademark owner. All trademarks and brands within this book are for clarifying purposes only and are the owned by the owners themselves, not affiliated with this document.

Table of Contents

Chapter 1

Introduction to Effective Communication

The Importance of Communication in Everyday Life

Communication is the invisible thread that weaves through the fabric of our daily lives, connecting us to the world and to each other. It is the cornerstone of human interaction, a vital skill that influences every aspect of our existence. From the moment we wake up and greet our loved ones to the time we spend negotiating deals at work or sharing stories with friends, communication is at the heart of it all. Its importance cannot be overstated, as it shapes our relationships, our careers, and our personal growth.

In the realm of personal relationships, communication serves as the bridge that connects individuals, allowing them to share thoughts, emotions, and experiences. It is through communication that we express love, resolve conflicts, and build trust. Imagine a world where words are left unspoken, where misunderstandings fester and relationships crumble. Effective communication is the antidote to such scenarios, fostering understanding and empathy. It enables us to articulate our needs and desires, to listen actively to others, and to respond with compassion. In doing so, it strengthens the bonds that hold us together, creating a sense of belonging and mutual respect.

In the professional sphere, communication is equally crucial. It is the lifeblood of any organization, facilitating the flow of information and ideas. Whether it's a team meeting, a presentation, or a simple email, the ability to convey messages clearly and persuasively can make the difference between success and failure. Effective communicators are often seen as leaders, as they possess the skills to inspire and motivate others. They can articulate a vision, rally support, and drive change. In a world where collaboration and innovation are key, communication is the tool that unlocks potential and propels us forward.

Beyond personal and professional realms, communication plays a pivotal role in our broader society. It is the means by which cultures are shared, traditions are passed down, and communities are built. Through communication, we engage in dialogue, debate, and discourse, shaping public opinion and influencing policy. It is the foundation of democracy, allowing citizens to voice their concerns and participate in decision-making processes. In an increasingly interconnected world, the ability to communicate across cultural and linguistic boundaries is more important than ever. It fosters understanding and cooperation, paving the way for a more harmonious and inclusive global community.

The importance of communication extends to our personal development as well. It is through communication that we learn and grow, acquiring new knowledge and skills. It challenges us to think critically, to question assumptions, and to explore new perspectives. By engaging in meaningful conversations, we expand our horizons and deepen our understanding of the world. Communication also plays a key role in self-expression, allowing us to articulate our thoughts and emotions. It is a powerful tool for self-reflection and introspection, helping us to gain insight into our own beliefs and values.

Despite its significance, communication is often taken for granted. We assume that because we can speak and listen, we are effective communicators. However, true communication requires more than just the exchange of words. It demands active listening, empathy, and the ability to adapt our message to different audiences. It involves being aware of nonverbal cues, such as body language and tone of voice, which can convey meaning beyond words. It requires clarity and precision, ensuring that our message is understood as intended. In essence, effective communication is a skill that must be cultivated and refined.

The barriers to effective communication are numerous and varied. They can stem from differences in language, culture, or background, leading to misunderstandings and misinterpretations. Emotional barriers, such as fear or anxiety, can hinder our ability to express ourselves openly and honestly. Physical barriers, such as noise or distance, can disrupt the flow of communication. To overcome these obstacles, we must be mindful of our own biases and assumptions, and strive to create an environment of openness and trust. By doing so, we can foster a culture of effective communication, where ideas are shared freely and collaboration thrives.

In the digital age, communication has taken on new forms and dimensions. The rise of social media and instant messaging has transformed the way we connect with others, offering new opportunities and challenges. On one hand, technology has made communication more accessible and convenient, allowing us to reach a global audience with the click of a button. On the other hand, it has introduced new complexities, such as the potential for miscommunication and the loss of personal touch. As we navigate this digital landscape, it is important to remain mindful of the principles of effective communication, ensuring that our messages are clear, respectful, and meaningful.

Understanding the Basics: What Makes Communication Effective?

Effective communication is an intricate dance of words, gestures, and emotions, a symphony that requires harmony between the sender and the receiver. At its core, effective communication is about ensuring that the intended message is not only delivered but also understood as intended. This understanding is the bedrock upon which successful interactions are built, whether in personal relationships, professional settings, or broader societal contexts.

The essence of effective communication lies in clarity. Clarity ensures that the message is conveyed without ambiguity, leaving little room for misinterpretation. This involves choosing words carefully, structuring sentences logically, and avoiding jargon that might confuse the listener. A clear message is like a well-lit path, guiding the listener to the intended destination without detours or dead ends. It requires the communicator to be mindful of their audience, tailoring their language and tone to suit the listener's level of understanding and cultural background.

Active listening is another cornerstone of effective communication. It is not merely about hearing the words spoken but about engaging with them fully. Active listening involves paying attention to the speaker, acknowledging their message, and responding thoughtfully. It requires the listener to set aside distractions, maintain eye contact, and provide feedback through nods or verbal affirmations. By doing so, the listener demonstrates respect and empathy, creating a space where open and honest dialogue can flourish.

Nonverbal communication plays a significant role in the effectiveness of our interactions. Body language, facial expressions, and gestures can convey meaning beyond words, adding depth and nuance to the message. A smile can signal warmth and friendliness, while crossed arms might indicate defensiveness or discomfort. Understanding these cues allows communicators to align their verbal and nonverbal messages, ensuring consistency and reinforcing the intended message. It also enables them to read the emotions and intentions of others, facilitating a more empathetic and responsive interaction.

The ability to adapt one's communication style to different contexts and audiences is a hallmark of effective communicators. This adaptability involves recognizing the unique needs and preferences of the listener and adjusting the message accordingly. In a professional setting, this might mean adopting a more formal tone and using industry-specific terminology. In a casual conversation with friends, it might involve using humor and colloquial language. By being flexible and responsive, communicators can build rapport and foster a sense of connection with their audience.

Feedback is an essential component of effective communication, serving as a mechanism for continuous improvement and mutual understanding. It involves both giving and receiving constructive criticism, allowing communicators to refine their message and approach. Feedback should be specific, focused on behavior rather than personality, and delivered in a respectful manner. It provides an opportunity for reflection and growth, enabling communicators to learn from their experiences and enhance their skills over time.

Empathy is the ability to understand and share the feelings of others, and it is a powerful tool in effective communication. By putting themselves in the shoes of the listener, communicators can anticipate their needs, concerns, and reactions. This empathetic approach fosters trust and openness, encouraging the listener to engage more fully in the conversation. It also helps communicators to navigate sensitive topics with care and consideration, minimizing the risk of conflict or misunderstanding.

The context in which communication occurs can significantly impact its effectiveness. Factors such as the physical environment, cultural norms, and the relationship between the communicators all play a role in shaping the interaction. Being aware of these contextual elements allows communicators to adjust their approach and create a conducive atmosphere for dialogue. For example, a quiet, private setting might be more appropriate for discussing personal matters, while a formal meeting room might be better suited for professional negotiations.

Emotional intelligence, the ability to recognize and manage one's emotions and the emotions of others, is a critical skill for effective communication. It involves being aware of emotional triggers, regulating emotional responses, and using emotions to enhance the communication process. By harnessing emotional intelligence, communicators can navigate complex interactions with grace and poise, maintaining composure and clarity even in challenging situations.

The timing of communication can also influence its effectiveness. Delivering a message at the right moment can enhance its impact, while poor timing can undermine its reception. Effective communicators are attuned to the rhythms of conversation, knowing when to speak and when to listen. They are sensitive to the emotional state of the listener, choosing moments when the listener is most receptive and open to the message.

Barriers to Effective Communication

Barriers to effective communication can be likened to invisible walls that obstruct the free flow of ideas and understanding between individuals. These barriers can arise from a multitude of sources, each contributing to the breakdown of communication in unique ways. Recognizing and addressing these barriers is crucial for fostering clear and meaningful interactions.

One of the most prevalent barriers is language. Language differences can create significant challenges, especially in multicultural settings where individuals may speak different native languages or dialects. Even when a common language is shared, variations in vocabulary, slang, and idiomatic expressions can lead to misunderstandings. For instance, a phrase that is innocuous in one culture might carry a completely different connotation in another. To overcome this barrier, communicators must strive for simplicity and clarity, avoiding jargon and complex language that might confuse the listener. Additionally, being open to asking for clarification and providing explanations can bridge the gap created by language differences.

Cultural differences extend beyond language and encompass a wide range of factors, including values, beliefs, and social norms. These differences can influence how messages are interpreted and how individuals interact with one another. For example, in some cultures, direct eye contact is a sign of confidence and honesty, while in others, it may be perceived as disrespectful or confrontational. Understanding and respecting cultural nuances is essential for effective communication. This requires a willingness to learn about and adapt to different cultural practices, as well as an openness to diverse perspectives.

Emotional barriers can also impede communication. Emotions such as anger, fear, or anxiety can cloud judgment and hinder the ability to convey or receive messages accurately. When emotions run high, individuals may become defensive, aggressive, or withdrawn, making it difficult to engage in constructive dialogue. To address emotional barriers, it is important to create a safe and supportive environment where individuals feel comfortable expressing their feelings. Active listening, empathy, and patience are key tools for navigating emotionally charged conversations and fostering mutual understanding.

Physical barriers, though often overlooked, can have a significant impact on communication. These barriers include environmental factors such as noise, distance, and physical obstructions that interfere with the transmission of messages. For instance, a conversation held in a noisy room may result in missed words or misinterpretations. Similarly, communicating over long distances, whether through digital means or across a crowded room, can lead to a loss of nuance and context. To mitigate physical barriers, communicators should strive to create an environment conducive to clear communication, whether by choosing a quiet location, using technology effectively, or ensuring that visual and auditory signals are unobstructed.

Psychological barriers are internal factors that affect how individuals perceive and process information. These barriers can include preconceived notions, biases, and stereotypes that influence how messages are interpreted. For example, if an individual holds a negative stereotype about a particular group, they may be less receptive to messages from members of that group. Overcoming psychological barriers requires self-awareness and a commitment to challenging one's own assumptions and biases. By approaching communication with an open mind and a willingness to consider alternative viewpoints, individuals can break down these internal barriers and engage in more meaningful interactions.

Perceptual barriers arise from differences in how individuals perceive and interpret the world around them. These differences can be influenced by factors such as past experiences, education, and personal beliefs. For instance, two people may witness the same event but interpret it in entirely different ways based on their unique perspectives. To address perceptual barriers, communicators should seek to understand the perspectives of others and acknowledge that multiple interpretations of a situation can coexist. This involves asking questions, seeking clarification, and being open to feedback.

Technological barriers have become increasingly relevant in today's digital age, where communication often takes place through electronic means. While technology offers numerous benefits, it can also introduce challenges such as misinterpretation of tone, lack of nonverbal cues, and information overload. For example, an email or text message may be misread as curt or impolite due to the absence of vocal inflections and facial expressions. To overcome technological barriers, communicators should be mindful of their tone and language when using digital platforms and consider supplementing written communication with verbal or face-to-face interactions when possible.

Organizational barriers are structural factors within an organization that hinder effective communication. These can include hierarchical structures, rigid protocols, and a lack of transparency. In organizations with strict hierarchies, information may become distorted as it travels through various levels, leading to misunderstandings and miscommunication. To address organizational barriers, it is important to foster a culture of open communication, where information flows freely and employees feel empowered to share their ideas and concerns. This can be achieved through regular feedback mechanisms, open-door policies, and collaborative decision-making processes.

Attitudinal barriers stem from individual attitudes and behaviors that negatively impact communication. These can include arrogance, defensiveness, and a lack of willingness to listen. For example, an individual who believes they are always right may dismiss the opinions of others, leading to a breakdown in communication. To overcome attitudinal barriers, individuals must cultivate a mindset of humility and openness, recognizing that effective communication is a two-way street that requires active participation and respect for diverse perspectives.

The Role of Nonverbal Communication

Nonverbal communication is an intricate dance of gestures, expressions, and postures that often speaks louder than words. It is a silent language that conveys emotions, intentions, and meanings, sometimes more powerfully than verbal communication. Understanding the role of nonverbal cues is essential for effective interaction, as it can enhance or undermine the spoken word.

Facial expressions are among the most universal forms of nonverbal communication. A smile can convey warmth and friendliness, while a frown may indicate displeasure or confusion. These expressions are often instinctive and can reveal true feelings, even when words attempt to mask them. For instance, a person may verbally express agreement, but a furrowed brow or pursed lips might suggest underlying skepticism. Recognizing and interpreting these subtle cues can provide valuable insights into a person's emotional state and intentions.

Gestures, too, play a significant role in communication. They can emphasize a point, illustrate an idea, or convey a message without the need for words. A thumbs-up can signal approval, while a wave can serve as a greeting or farewell.

However, gestures can vary widely across cultures, and what is considered positive in one culture may be offensive in another. For example, the "OK" hand gesture is a sign of approval in many Western cultures but can be interpreted as an insult in parts of the Middle East. Being aware of cultural differences in gestures is crucial for avoiding misunderstandings and fostering respectful communication.

Posture and body orientation are other critical components of nonverbal communication. The way individuals position themselves can indicate their level of engagement, confidence, or openness. An open posture, with arms uncrossed and body facing the speaker, suggests attentiveness and receptivity. Conversely, a closed posture, with arms crossed and body turned away, may signal defensiveness or disinterest. In a professional setting, maintaining an upright posture can convey confidence and authority, while slouching may be perceived as a lack of interest or professionalism.

Eye contact is a powerful nonverbal cue that can convey a range of emotions and intentions. It can signal confidence, sincerity, and attentiveness, or it can be used to assert dominance or challenge authority. In many Western cultures, maintaining eye contact is seen as a sign of respect and engagement, while in some Asian cultures, prolonged eye contact may be considered disrespectful or confrontational. Understanding the cultural context of eye contact is essential for effective communication, as it can influence how messages are received and interpreted.

Proxemics, or the study of personal space, is another important aspect of nonverbal communication. The distance individuals maintain between themselves and others can convey intimacy, aggression, or formality. In general, people tend to stand closer to those they feel comfortable with and maintain more distance from strangers or authority figures. However, cultural norms regarding personal space can vary significantly. In some cultures, close physical proximity is a sign of friendliness and warmth, while in others, it may be perceived as intrusive or disrespectful. Being mindful of personal space preferences can help prevent discomfort and foster positive interactions.

Touch is a nuanced form of nonverbal communication that can convey a wide range of emotions, from affection and support to aggression and dominance. A handshake can establish rapport and trust, while a pat on the back can offer encouragement or congratulations. However, the appropriateness of touch varies across cultures and contexts. In some cultures, physical touch is a common and accepted form of communication, while in others, it may be reserved for close relationships or specific situations. Understanding the cultural and situational context of touch is crucial for ensuring that it is perceived as respectful and appropriate.

Paralanguage, or the vocal elements that accompany speech, is another key component of nonverbal communication. This includes tone, pitch, volume, and rate of speech, all of which can influence how a message is perceived. A warm, friendly tone can convey approachability and empathy, while a harsh, loud tone may be perceived as aggressive or confrontational. Similarly, speaking too quickly may suggest nervousness or impatience, while speaking too slowly may be interpreted as condescension or disinterest. Being aware of paralanguage and its impact on communication can help individuals convey their messages more effectively and avoid unintended misunderstandings.

Nonverbal communication also plays a crucial role in conveying emotions and building rapport in interpersonal relationships. It can reinforce verbal messages, add depth and nuance to interactions, and help establish trust and connection. For example, a comforting touch or empathetic facial expression can provide reassurance and support in times of distress, while a genuine smile can foster a sense of camaraderie and goodwill. By being attuned to nonverbal cues, individuals can enhance their emotional intelligence and improve their ability to connect with others on a deeper level.

In professional settings, nonverbal communication can influence perceptions of competence, credibility, and leadership. A confident posture, steady eye contact, and appropriate gestures can enhance a speaker's authority and persuasiveness, while incongruent or negative nonverbal cues can undermine their message. For instance, a speaker who avoids eye contact or fidgets nervously may be perceived as lacking confidence or credibility, regardless of the content of their message. By mastering nonverbal communication skills, professionals can enhance their effectiveness as communicators and leaders.

Despite its importance, nonverbal communication is often overlooked or misunderstood. Many individuals are unaware of the nonverbal signals they send or how they are perceived by others. Developing an awareness of one's own nonverbal communication and learning to interpret the cues of others can significantly enhance interpersonal interactions. This requires practice, observation, and a willingness to seek feedback and make adjustments as needed.

Setting Your Communication Goals

Active listening is a skill that transcends mere hearing, transforming communication into a dynamic and engaging exchange. It involves fully concentrating, understanding, responding, and remembering what is being said. This art form is not just about the words spoken but also about the emotions and intentions behind them. Mastering active listening can enhance personal and professional relationships, foster empathy, and lead to more effective problem-solving.

Imagine a conversation as a dance, where both partners must be in sync to create a harmonious flow. Active listening is the rhythm that guides this dance, ensuring that each step is purposeful and meaningful. It requires the listener to be present, both mentally and emotionally, setting aside distractions and preconceived notions. This presence allows for a deeper connection with the speaker, creating a space where genuine understanding can flourish.

One of the fundamental components of active listening is giving undivided attention. In a world filled with constant distractions, this can be a challenging task. However, by consciously choosing to focus on the speaker, you demonstrate respect and interest in their message. This can be achieved by maintaining eye contact, nodding in acknowledgment, and using verbal affirmations such as "I see" or "I understand." These small gestures convey that you are engaged and invested in the conversation.

Empathy plays a crucial role in active listening. It involves putting yourself in the speaker's shoes and trying to understand their perspective. This requires an open mind and a willingness to set aside your own biases and judgments. By approaching the conversation with empathy, you create an environment where the speaker feels heard and valued. This not only strengthens the relationship but also encourages open and honest communication.

Reflective listening is another key aspect of active listening. It involves paraphrasing or summarizing what the speaker has said to ensure understanding. This technique serves two purposes: it confirms that you have accurately interpreted the message, and it provides the speaker with an opportunity to clarify any misunderstandings. For example, you might say, "So what I'm hearing is that you're feeling overwhelmed with your workload. Is that correct?" This not only demonstrates that you are actively engaged but also fosters a collaborative dialogue.

Asking open-ended questions is a powerful tool in active listening. These questions encourage the speaker to elaborate on their thoughts and feelings, providing deeper insights into their perspective. Instead of asking yes or no questions, opt for inquiries that begin with "how," "what," or "why." For instance, "What led you to that conclusion?" or "How did that experience make you feel?" These questions invite the speaker to share more, enriching the conversation and enhancing understanding.

Nonverbal communication is an often-overlooked element of active listening. Body language, facial expressions, and gestures can convey a wealth of information and significantly impact the quality of the interaction. Being mindful of your own nonverbal cues, as well as those of the speaker, can provide valuable insights into the emotions and intentions behind the words. For example, crossed arms may indicate defensiveness, while a relaxed posture can signal openness and receptivity.

Silence is a powerful yet underutilized aspect of active listening. Allowing pauses in the conversation gives the speaker time to reflect and gather their thoughts, leading to more thoughtful and meaningful exchanges. It also provides you with an opportunity to process the information and formulate a considered response. Embracing silence can create a sense of calm and patience, fostering a deeper connection between the speaker and listener.

Active listening is not a passive activity; it requires conscious effort and practice. Developing this skill involves being aware of your listening habits and making intentional changes to improve them. Start by setting small, achievable goals, such as focusing on one conversation per day where you practice active listening techniques. Over time, these habits will become second nature, enhancing your ability to connect with others on a deeper level.

The benefits of active listening extend beyond individual interactions. In a professional setting, it can lead to more effective teamwork, improved problem-solving, and increased productivity. By fostering an environment where everyone feels heard and valued, you create a culture of collaboration and innovation. In personal relationships, active listening can strengthen bonds, build trust, and promote mutual understanding.

Chapter 2

Building a Strong Foundation: Listening Skills

The Art of Active Listening

Active listening is a transformative skill that elevates communication from a mere exchange of words to a profound connection between individuals. It involves more than just hearing; it requires a conscious effort to understand, interpret, and respond to the messages conveyed by others. This skill is essential in both personal and professional settings, as it fosters empathy, builds trust, and enhances relationships.

Consider a scenario where two colleagues are discussing a project. One is explaining their ideas, while the other is nodding along, seemingly attentive. However, the listener's mind is elsewhere, preoccupied with their own thoughts and concerns. This is a common occurrence, where the act of listening is superficial, lacking genuine engagement. Active listening, on the other hand, demands full presence and attention, creating a space where meaningful dialogue can thrive.

The foundation of active listening lies in giving undivided attention to the speaker. This means setting aside distractions, such as electronic devices or wandering thoughts, and focusing entirely on the conversation at hand. Eye contact is a powerful tool in this regard, as it signals to the speaker that you are engaged and interested in what they have to say. Additionally, maintaining an open and receptive posture can further convey your attentiveness and willingness to listen.

Empathy is a cornerstone of active listening. It involves stepping into the speaker's shoes and viewing the world from their perspective. This requires an open mind and a suspension of judgment, allowing you to fully appreciate the speaker's emotions and experiences. By cultivating empathy, you create an environment where the speaker feels understood and valued, encouraging them to share more openly and honestly.

Reflective listening is a technique that enhances understanding and clarity. It involves paraphrasing or summarizing the speaker's message to confirm your interpretation. For example, you might say, "It sounds like you're feeling frustrated with the current situation. Is that right?" This not only demonstrates that you are actively engaged but also provides the speaker with an opportunity to clarify any misunderstandings. Reflective listening fosters a collaborative dialogue, where both parties work together to achieve mutual understanding.

Asking open-ended questions is another effective strategy in active listening. These questions invite the speaker to elaborate on their thoughts and feelings, providing deeper insights into their perspective. Instead of asking questions that can be answered with a simple yes or no, opt for inquiries that begin with "how," "what," or "why." For instance, "What challenges are you facing with this project?" or "How did that experience impact you?" These questions encourage the speaker to share more, enriching the conversation and enhancing understanding.

Nonverbal communication plays a significant role in active listening. Body language, facial expressions, and gestures can convey a wealth of information and significantly impact the quality of the interaction. Being mindful of your own nonverbal cues, as well as those of the speaker, can provide valuable insights into the emotions and intentions behind the words. For example, a furrowed brow may indicate confusion, while a smile can signal agreement or understanding.

Silence is a powerful yet often underappreciated aspect of active listening. Allowing pauses in the conversation gives the speaker time to reflect and gather their thoughts, leading to more thoughtful and meaningful exchanges. It also provides you with an opportunity to process the information and formulate a considered response. Embracing silence can create a sense of calm and patience, fostering a deeper connection between the speaker and listener.

Active listening is not a passive activity; it requires conscious effort and practice. Developing this skill involves being aware of your listening habits and making intentional changes to improve them. Start by setting small, achievable goals, such as focusing on one conversation per day where you practice active listening techniques. Over time, these habits will become second nature, enhancing your ability to connect with others on a deeper level.

The benefits of active listening extend beyond individual interactions. In a professional setting, it can lead to more effective teamwork, improved problem-solving, and increased productivity. By fostering an environment where everyone feels heard and valued, you create a culture of collaboration and innovation. In personal relationships, active listening can strengthen bonds, build trust, and promote mutual understanding.

Overcoming Listening Barriers

Listening is an essential component of effective communication, yet it is often hindered by various barriers that can impede understanding and connection. These barriers can be internal or external, conscious or unconscious, and they can significantly impact the quality of our interactions. Recognizing and overcoming these obstacles is crucial for fostering meaningful dialogue and building stronger relationships.

One of the most common barriers to listening is the presence of internal distractions. Our minds are constantly buzzing with thoughts, concerns, and to-do lists, which can easily divert our attention away from the speaker. This mental noise can prevent us from fully engaging in the conversation, leading to misunderstandings and missed opportunities for connection. To combat this, it is important to practice mindfulness and focus on being present in the moment. By consciously setting aside distractions and directing our attention to the speaker, we can create a mental space that is conducive to active listening.

Preconceived notions and biases also pose significant challenges to effective listening. These mental filters shape our perceptions and interpretations of what we hear, often leading us to make assumptions or judgments before fully understanding the speaker's message. This can result in a distorted view of the conversation and hinder our ability to empathize with the speaker. To overcome this barrier, it is essential to approach each conversation with an open mind and a willingness to challenge our own assumptions. By actively seeking to understand the speaker's perspective, we can foster a more inclusive and empathetic dialogue.

Emotional reactions can also interfere with our ability to listen effectively. When a speaker's words trigger strong emotions, such as anger, frustration, or defensiveness, it can be difficult to remain objective and attentive. These emotions can cloud our judgment and lead us to react impulsively, rather than responding thoughtfully. To manage emotional barriers, it is important to develop emotional intelligence and self-awareness. By recognizing our emotional triggers and learning to regulate our responses, we can maintain our composure and focus on the speaker's message.

External distractions, such as noise, interruptions, or environmental factors, can also impede our ability to listen. These distractions can divert our attention away from the speaker and disrupt the flow of the conversation. To minimize external barriers, it is important to create a conducive listening environment. This may involve finding a quiet space, minimizing background noise, or setting boundaries to prevent interruptions. By taking proactive steps to reduce external distractions, we can enhance our ability to listen and engage with the speaker.

Language and cultural differences can also present challenges to effective listening. Variations in language, dialect, or cultural norms can lead to misunderstandings or misinterpretations of the speaker's message. To bridge these gaps, it is important to cultivate cultural competence and sensitivity. This involves being aware of and respectful towards cultural differences, as well as seeking clarification when needed. By approaching conversations with curiosity and a willingness to learn, we can overcome language and cultural barriers and foster more inclusive communication.

Another barrier to listening is the tendency to focus on formulating a response rather than truly understanding the speaker's message. This can lead to superficial listening, where we hear the words but fail to grasp the underlying meaning or emotions. To counteract this tendency, it is important to prioritize understanding over responding. By actively listening and seeking to comprehend the speaker's perspective, we can engage in more meaningful and authentic dialogue.

Time constraints and pressure can also hinder our ability to listen effectively. In fast-paced environments, we may feel rushed or overwhelmed, leading us to prioritize efficiency over understanding. This can result in hurried conversations and missed opportunities for connection. To address this barrier, it is important to allocate sufficient time for meaningful interactions and prioritize quality over quantity. By valuing the importance of listening and dedicating time to it, we can enhance our communication and build stronger relationships.

Techniques for Better Listening

Listening is an art that requires more than just hearing words; it demands attention, empathy, and a genuine desire to understand. In a world where communication is often rushed and superficial, honing the skill of effective listening can transform interactions and deepen relationships. By employing specific techniques, one can become a more attentive and responsive listener, fostering an environment of trust and mutual respect.

One fundamental technique for better listening is active engagement. This involves fully immersing oneself in the conversation, both mentally and physically. Maintaining eye contact, nodding in acknowledgment, and using verbal affirmations such as "I see" or "I understand" can signal to the speaker that their message is being received and valued. This level of engagement not only encourages the speaker to share more openly but also helps the listener to stay focused and present.

Paraphrasing is another powerful tool in the listener's arsenal. By restating the speaker's message in one's own words, the listener can confirm their understanding and clarify any potential misunderstandings. This technique not only demonstrates attentiveness but also provides an opportunity for the speaker to correct any inaccuracies or elaborate on their points. Paraphrasing can be particularly useful in complex or emotionally charged conversations, where nuances may be easily overlooked.

Empathy plays a crucial role in effective listening. By putting oneself in the speaker's shoes and attempting to understand their emotions and perspectives, the listener can create a more compassionate and supportive dialogue. This involves not only hearing the words but also paying attention to the speaker's tone, body language, and emotional cues. Empathetic listening fosters a sense of connection and validation, encouraging the speaker to express themselves more freely.

Asking open-ended questions is another technique that can enhance listening skills. These questions invite the speaker to share more detailed and expansive responses, providing deeper insights into their thoughts and feelings. By avoiding questions that can be answered with a simple "yes" or "no," the listener can encourage a more dynamic and engaging conversation. This approach not only enriches the dialogue but also demonstrates a genuine interest in the speaker's perspective.

Silence, often overlooked, is a powerful component of effective listening. Allowing pauses in the conversation gives the speaker time to reflect and articulate their thoughts more clearly. It also provides the listener with an opportunity to process the information and formulate thoughtful responses. Embracing silence can prevent the conversation from becoming rushed or superficial, allowing for a more meaningful exchange.

Nonverbal communication is an integral aspect of listening that should not be underestimated. Body language, facial expressions, and gestures can convey attentiveness and understanding, often more powerfully than words. By aligning nonverbal cues with verbal affirmations, the listener can create a cohesive and supportive listening environment. This alignment reinforces the speaker's sense of being heard and respected.

Reflective listening is a technique that involves mirroring the speaker's emotions and sentiments. By acknowledging and validating the speaker's feelings, the listener can create a safe space for open and honest communication. This technique is particularly effective in emotionally charged situations, where the speaker may feel vulnerable or misunderstood.

Reflective listening demonstrates empathy and compassion, fostering a deeper connection between the speaker and listener.

Practicing patience is essential for effective listening. In a fast-paced world, there is often a tendency to rush conversations or interrupt the speaker. However, true listening requires patience and a willingness to allow the conversation to unfold naturally. By resisting the urge to interject or offer solutions prematurely, the listener can create a more respectful and considerate dialogue. This patience not only benefits the speaker but also allows the listener to gain a more comprehensive understanding of the message.

Self-awareness is a critical component of effective listening. By recognizing one's own biases, assumptions, and emotional triggers, the listener can approach the conversation with an open mind and a willingness to learn. This self-awareness enables the listener to set aside preconceived notions and focus on the speaker's message, fostering a more authentic and unbiased dialogue.

Finally, practicing mindfulness can enhance listening skills by promoting presence and focus. By cultivating a mindful approach to listening, the listener can become more attuned to the speaker's words and emotions, reducing the impact of internal and external distractions. Mindfulness encourages the listener to remain present in the moment, creating a more attentive and engaged listening experience.

Listening with Empathy and Understanding

Empathy and understanding are the cornerstones of effective communication, transforming mere exchanges of words into meaningful connections. Listening with empathy involves more than just hearing the speaker's words; it requires an emotional resonance that acknowledges and validates their feelings and perspectives. This chapter delves into the nuances of empathetic listening, offering practical techniques to cultivate this essential skill.

At the heart of empathetic listening lies the ability to suspend judgment and approach the conversation with an open mind. This means setting aside preconceived notions and biases, allowing the speaker's words to be received without the filter of personal opinions. By doing so, the listener creates a safe space where the speaker feels free to express themselves without fear of criticism or dismissal. This openness fosters a sense of trust and encourages more honest and vulnerable communication.

One effective technique for listening with empathy is to focus on the speaker's emotions rather than just the content of their message. This involves paying attention to the speaker's tone, body language, and facial expressions, which often convey more about their emotional state than words alone. By tuning into these nonverbal cues, the listener can gain a deeper understanding of the speaker's feelings and respond in a way that acknowledges and validates those emotions.

Reflective listening is a powerful tool for demonstrating empathy. This technique involves mirroring the speaker's emotions and sentiments, allowing them to feel heard and understood. For example, if a speaker expresses frustration, the listener might respond with, "It sounds like you're feeling really frustrated about this situation." This reflection not only shows that the listener is paying attention but also provides an opportunity for the speaker to clarify or expand on their feelings.

Another key aspect of empathetic listening is the ability to ask open-ended questions that encourage the speaker to share more about their experiences and emotions. These questions invite the speaker to elaborate on their thoughts and feelings, providing the listener with a richer understanding of their perspective. By avoiding questions that can be answered with a simple "yes" or "no," the listener can create a more dynamic and engaging conversation that fosters empathy and connection.

Practicing patience is essential when listening with empathy. In a world where conversations are often rushed, taking the time to fully engage with the speaker's message can make a significant difference. This means allowing the speaker to express themselves at their own pace, without interrupting or rushing to offer solutions. By demonstrating patience, the listener shows respect for the speaker's process and creates a more supportive and understanding environment.

Empathetic listening also involves acknowledging and validating the speaker's feelings, even if they differ from one's own. This requires the listener to set aside their own emotions and focus on the speaker's experience. By doing so, the listener can offer genuine support and understanding, reinforcing the speaker's sense of being heard and valued. This validation can be as simple as saying, "I can see why you would feel that way," or "That sounds really challenging."

Self-awareness plays a crucial role in empathetic listening. By recognizing one's own emotional triggers and biases, the listener can approach the conversation with greater objectivity and empathy. This self-awareness allows the listener to remain present and focused on the speaker's message, rather than becoming distracted by their own thoughts or emotions. By cultivating self-awareness, the listener can create a more authentic and empathetic connection with the speaker.

Mindfulness is another valuable practice for enhancing empathetic listening skills. By being fully present in the moment, the listener can become more attuned to the speaker's words and emotions, reducing the impact of internal and external distractions. Mindfulness encourages the listener to remain focused on the speaker's message, creating a more attentive and engaged listening experience. This presence not only benefits the listener but also empowers the speaker to express themselves more openly and authentically.

Empathetic listening can be particularly challenging in emotionally charged situations, where the speaker may feel vulnerable or misunderstood. In these instances, it is important for the listener to remain calm and composed, offering a steady and supportive presence. By maintaining a compassionate and empathetic demeanor, the listener can help to de-escalate tension and create a more constructive dialogue.

Finally, it is important to remember that empathetic listening is a skill that requires practice and dedication. By consistently applying these techniques in daily interactions, the listener can gradually develop a more empathetic and understanding approach to communication. This not only enhances the quality of conversations but also strengthens relationships and fosters a deeper sense of connection and trust.

The Impact of Listening on Relationships

Listening is an art that holds the power to transform relationships, whether they are personal, professional, or casual. The impact of listening on relationships is profound, as it fosters understanding, trust, and connection between individuals. When people feel heard, they are more likely to open up, share their thoughts and emotions, and engage in meaningful dialogue. This chapter delves into the various ways in which listening can influence relationships, offering insights and practical advice for harnessing this powerful tool.

At the core of any strong relationship lies effective communication, and listening is a fundamental component of this process. When individuals actively listen to one another, they demonstrate respect and validation for the other person's perspective. This validation is crucial, as it reinforces the speaker's sense of self-worth and encourages them to continue sharing their thoughts and feelings.

In turn, this openness fosters a deeper connection between the individuals involved, strengthening the bond that holds the relationship together.

One of the most significant impacts of listening on relationships is the development of trust. Trust is built when individuals feel confident that their thoughts and emotions will be received with empathy and understanding. By consistently practicing active listening, individuals can create an environment where trust can flourish. This trust serves as a foundation for the relationship, allowing it to withstand challenges and grow over time. When trust is present, individuals are more likely to engage in honest and open communication, further enhancing the quality of the relationship.

Listening also plays a crucial role in conflict resolution within relationships. Disagreements and misunderstandings are inevitable, but how they are handled can make all the difference. By actively listening to the other person's perspective during a conflict, individuals can gain a better understanding of the underlying issues and work towards a resolution that satisfies both parties. This approach not only helps to resolve the immediate conflict but also strengthens the relationship by demonstrating a commitment to understanding and addressing each other's needs.

Empathy is another key element that is enhanced through listening. When individuals listen with empathy, they are able to put themselves in the other person's shoes and gain insight into their emotions and experiences. This empathetic understanding fosters compassion and support, which are essential for nurturing healthy relationships. By cultivating empathy through listening, individuals can create a more harmonious and supportive environment, where both parties feel valued and understood.

In professional settings, listening can have a significant impact on workplace relationships and dynamics. Effective listening skills can enhance collaboration and teamwork, as individuals feel more comfortable sharing their ideas and opinions. This open exchange of information can lead to increased creativity and innovation, as diverse perspectives are considered and integrated into decision-making processes. Furthermore, when leaders demonstrate strong listening skills, they inspire confidence and loyalty among their team members, creating a more cohesive and motivated workforce.

Listening also plays a vital role in personal relationships, such as those with family and friends. By actively listening to loved ones, individuals can strengthen their emotional bonds and create a sense of closeness and intimacy. This connection is particularly important during times of stress or difficulty, as it provides a source of support and comfort. By being present and attentive, individuals can offer reassurance and understanding, helping to alleviate feelings of isolation and loneliness.

In romantic relationships, listening is essential for maintaining a strong and healthy partnership. Couples who prioritize listening are better equipped to navigate the complexities of their relationship, as they are more attuned to each other's needs and emotions. This attentiveness fosters a sense of security and stability, allowing the relationship to thrive. By consistently practicing active listening, couples can deepen their emotional connection and create a lasting bond built on mutual respect and understanding.

The impact of listening on relationships extends beyond individual interactions, influencing the broader social fabric of communities and societies. When individuals practice active listening, they contribute to a culture of empathy and understanding, where diverse perspectives are valued and respected. This cultural shift can lead to more inclusive and harmonious communities, where individuals feel empowered to share their voices and contribute to collective decision-making processes.

To harness the power of listening in relationships, individuals can adopt several practical strategies. First, it is important to create a conducive environment for listening, free from distractions and interruptions. This means setting aside dedicated time for conversations and ensuring that both parties feel comfortable and relaxed. By prioritizing the conversation, individuals demonstrate their commitment to listening and valuing the other person's perspective.

Active listening techniques, such as maintaining eye contact, nodding, and providing verbal affirmations, can also enhance the listening experience. These nonverbal cues signal to the speaker that their message is being received and understood, encouraging them to continue sharing. Additionally, paraphrasing and summarizing the speaker's message can help to clarify understanding and ensure that both parties are on the same page.

It is also important to approach conversations with an open mind and a willingness to learn. This means setting aside personal biases and judgments, allowing the speaker's message to be received without preconceived notions. By adopting a curious and inquisitive mindset, individuals can gain new insights and perspectives, enriching their understanding of the other person's experiences and emotions.

Finally, practicing patience and empathy is essential for effective listening. This means allowing the speaker to express themselves at their own pace, without rushing or interrupting. By demonstrating patience, individuals show respect for the speaker's process and create a more supportive and understanding environment. Empathy, on the other hand, involves putting oneself in the speaker's shoes and acknowledging their emotions and experiences. By cultivating empathy, individuals can create a more compassionate and connected relationship.

Chapter 3

Crafting Your Message: Verbal Communication

Choosing the Right Words: Language and Tone

Language and tone are the twin pillars of effective communication, shaping the way messages are received and interpreted. The words we choose and the tone we employ can either bridge gaps or create chasms in understanding. In any interaction, whether personal or professional, the ability to select the right words and tone can significantly influence the outcome of the conversation. This chapter delves into the nuances of language and tone, offering insights and practical advice for mastering these essential elements of communication.

The power of language lies in its ability to convey not just information, but also emotion and intent. Words are the building blocks of communication, and their selection can dramatically alter the meaning of a message. Consider the difference between saying "I need your help" and "I would appreciate your assistance." Both phrases convey a request for help, but the latter is more polite and considerate, potentially eliciting a more positive response. The choice of words can reflect respect, empathy, and understanding, or conversely, can come across as harsh, dismissive, or confrontational.

Tone, on the other hand, is the emotional coloring of language. It encompasses the attitude and feelings conveyed through speech or writing. A friendly tone can make even the most difficult conversations more palatable, while a harsh tone can escalate tensions and lead to misunderstandings. Tone is often conveyed through vocal inflections, body language, and even punctuation in written communication. For instance, a simple exclamation mark can transform a neutral statement into an enthusiastic one, while a question mark can introduce doubt or curiosity.

In personal relationships, the right language and tone can foster intimacy and trust. When communicating with loved ones, it's important to choose words that express care and consideration. This means being mindful of the impact that words can have on the other person's emotions and self-esteem. A supportive and encouraging tone can strengthen bonds and create a sense of security, while a critical or dismissive tone can erode trust and create distance.

In professional settings, language and tone play a crucial role in establishing credibility and authority. The ability to communicate clearly and confidently can enhance one's professional image and facilitate collaboration. This involves using precise and concise language, avoiding jargon or overly complex terms that may confuse the listener. A respectful and assertive tone can convey competence and inspire confidence, while an aggressive or passive tone can undermine one's message and credibility.

The cultural context also plays a significant role in determining the appropriateness of language and tone. Different cultures have varying norms and expectations regarding communication styles, and what may be considered polite or respectful in one culture may be perceived differently in another. Being aware of these cultural differences and adapting language and tone accordingly can enhance cross-cultural communication and prevent misunderstandings.

To effectively choose the right words and tone, it's important to consider the purpose and audience of the communication. This involves assessing the goals of the interaction and tailoring the language and tone to suit the context. For example, a formal tone may be appropriate for a business meeting, while a more casual tone may be suitable for a conversation with friends. Understanding the needs and preferences of the audience can guide the selection of language and tone, ensuring that the message is received as intended.

Active listening is another key component of effective communication, as it allows individuals to gauge the other person's response and adjust their language and tone accordingly. By paying attention to verbal and nonverbal cues, individuals can assess whether their message is being understood and whether any adjustments are needed. This dynamic process of feedback and adaptation can enhance the effectiveness of communication and build rapport between the parties involved.

Empathy is also essential for choosing the right words and tone. By putting oneself in the other person's shoes, individuals can gain insight into their emotions and perspectives, allowing them to tailor their language and tone to meet the other person's needs. This empathetic approach can create a more supportive and understanding environment, where both parties feel valued and respected.

In written communication, the choice of words and tone is equally important, as the absence of vocal inflections and body language can make it more challenging to convey emotion and intent. This requires careful consideration of word choice, sentence structure, and punctuation to ensure that the message is clear and accurately reflects the intended tone. For example, using positive language and avoiding negative or confrontational words can create a more constructive and collaborative tone.

The impact of language and tone extends beyond individual interactions, influencing the broader social and cultural landscape. The words and tone we use can shape perceptions, attitudes, and behaviors, contributing to the creation of inclusive and respectful communities. By choosing language and tone that promote understanding and empathy, individuals can contribute to a more harmonious and equitable society.

To master the art of choosing the right words and tone, individuals can adopt several practical strategies. First, it is important to expand one's vocabulary and develop a nuanced understanding of language. This involves reading widely, engaging in conversations, and seeking feedback to enhance one's linguistic skills. A rich vocabulary allows for more precise and effective communication, enabling individuals to convey their thoughts and emotions with clarity and impact.

Practicing mindfulness and self-awareness can also enhance one's ability to choose the right words and tone. This involves being attuned to one's own emotions and reactions, as well as those of the other person. By cultivating self-awareness, individuals can identify any biases or assumptions that may influence their language and tone, allowing them to communicate more authentically and empathetically.

Finally, seeking feedback and reflecting on past interactions can provide valuable insights into one's communication style and areas for improvement. By being open to constructive criticism and learning from experience, individuals can refine their ability to choose the right words and tone, enhancing their overall communication skills.

Structuring Your Message for Clarity

Crafting a message that resonates with clarity is akin to constructing a well-designed building. Each element must be meticulously planned and executed to ensure that the final structure stands firm and serves its intended purpose. The foundation of any clear message lies in its structure, which guides the audience through the content in a logical and coherent manner. This chapter delves into the art of structuring messages for clarity, offering practical strategies and insights to help beginners communicate effectively.

The first step in structuring a message is to define its purpose. Understanding the goal of the communication is crucial, as it informs the content and organization of the message. Whether the aim is to inform, persuade, entertain, or request action, having a clear purpose provides direction and focus.

This clarity of intent allows the communicator to prioritize information and eliminate unnecessary details that may obscure the message.

Once the purpose is established, identifying the key points to be conveyed is essential. These points form the backbone of the message and should be presented in a logical sequence that guides the audience through the content. Organizing information in a coherent manner helps the audience follow the argument or narrative, reducing the likelihood of confusion or misinterpretation. A well-structured message often follows a clear progression, with each point building on the previous one to create a cohesive whole.

To enhance clarity, it's important to use simple and direct language. Avoiding jargon, technical terms, or complex sentence structures can make the message more accessible to a wider audience. When technical language is necessary, providing clear definitions or explanations can aid understanding. The goal is to communicate ideas in a way that is easily digestible, allowing the audience to grasp the message without unnecessary effort.

In addition to language, the use of visual aids can significantly enhance the clarity of a message. Diagrams, charts, and images can help illustrate complex concepts, making them more tangible and easier to understand. Visual aids can also break up large blocks of text, providing visual interest and aiding retention. When incorporating visuals, it's important to ensure they are relevant and directly support the key points of the message.

The structure of a message can also be enhanced by using signposts and transitions. These linguistic tools guide the audience through the content, signaling shifts in topic or emphasis. Phrases such as "firstly," "in addition," and "on the other hand" can help clarify the relationship between different points, making the message easier to follow. Transitions create a smooth flow, allowing the audience to move seamlessly from one idea to the next.

Another effective strategy for structuring messages is to employ storytelling techniques. Stories have a natural structure that engages the audience and aids comprehension. By framing information within a narrative, communicators can create a more compelling and memorable message. Stories can also humanize abstract concepts, making them more relatable and easier to understand. When using storytelling, it's important to ensure that the narrative aligns with the purpose of the message and supports the key points.

Feedback is a valuable tool for refining the structure of a message. By seeking input from others, communicators can gain insights into how their message is perceived and identify areas for improvement. Feedback can highlight aspects of the message that may be unclear or confusing, allowing for adjustments to be made before the message is delivered to a wider audience. This iterative process of refinement can enhance the clarity and effectiveness of the message.

The context in which a message is delivered also plays a crucial role in its clarity. Understanding the audience's needs, preferences, and expectations can inform the structure and content of the message. Tailoring the message to suit the audience's level of knowledge and interest can enhance engagement and comprehension. Additionally, considering the medium of communication—whether written, spoken, or visual—can influence the structure and presentation of the message.

Practicing active listening is another key component of effective communication. By paying attention to the audience's responses and adjusting the message accordingly, communicators can enhance clarity and understanding. Active listening involves being attuned to verbal and nonverbal cues, allowing for real-time adjustments to the message. This dynamic process of interaction can create a more responsive and effective communication experience.

Empathy is also essential for structuring messages with clarity. By considering the audience's perspective and anticipating their questions or concerns, communicators can address potential misunderstandings before they arise. This empathetic approach can create a more inclusive and supportive communication environment, where the audience feels valued and understood.

To master the art of structuring messages for clarity, individuals can adopt several practical strategies. First, it is important to plan and outline the message before delivery. This involves identifying the key points, organizing them in a logical sequence, and considering the most effective way to present them. A well-thought-out plan provides a roadmap for the message, ensuring that it is clear and coherent.

Practicing mindfulness and self-awareness can also enhance one's ability to structure messages effectively. This involves being attuned to one's own communication style and identifying any habits or tendencies that may hinder clarity. By cultivating self-awareness, individuals can refine their communication skills and develop a more effective approach to structuring messages.

Finally, seeking feedback and reflecting on past interactions can provide valuable insights into one's communication style and areas for improvement. By being open to constructive criticism and learning from experience, individuals can refine their ability to structure messages with clarity, enhancing their overall communication skills.

The Power of Storytelling in Communication

Storytelling is an ancient art form that has been used for centuries to convey messages, share knowledge, and connect people across cultures and generations. Its power lies in its ability to engage, inspire, and persuade, making it an invaluable tool in communication. At its core, storytelling is about creating a narrative that resonates with the audience, evoking emotions and fostering a deeper understanding of the subject matter. This chapter explores the transformative power of storytelling in communication, offering insights and strategies for harnessing its potential.

One of the most compelling aspects of storytelling is its ability to capture attention. In a world saturated with information, grabbing and maintaining an audience's focus is a significant challenge. Stories have a unique way of drawing people in, creating a sense of curiosity and anticipation. By weaving a narrative, communicators can create an emotional connection with their audience, making the message more memorable and impactful. This emotional engagement is crucial, as it helps the audience relate to the content on a personal level, increasing the likelihood of retention and understanding.

The structure of a story plays a vital role in its effectiveness. A well-crafted narrative typically follows a clear arc, with a beginning, middle, and end. This structure provides a framework for organizing information, guiding the audience through the content in a logical and coherent manner. The beginning sets the stage, introducing the characters and context, while the middle develops the plot, presenting challenges and conflicts. The end resolves the narrative, offering insights or lessons learned. This progression creates a sense of completeness, allowing the audience to follow the story with ease and clarity.

Characters are another essential element of storytelling. They serve as the vehicle through which the audience experiences the narrative, providing a relatable and human perspective. By creating characters that the audience can identify with, communicators can foster empathy and understanding. Characters can be real or fictional, but they should be well-developed and multidimensional, with motivations and emotions that drive the narrative forward. Through characters, storytellers can explore complex ideas and themes, making them more accessible and relatable to the audience.

Conflict is a key component of any compelling story. It creates tension and drama, driving the narrative and keeping the audience engaged. Conflict can take many forms, from external challenges and obstacles to internal struggles and dilemmas. By presenting conflict, storytellers can explore different perspectives and highlight the complexities of the subject matter. This exploration of conflict can lead to deeper insights and understanding, as the audience is encouraged to consider different viewpoints and reflect on their own beliefs and values.

The use of vivid imagery and sensory details is another powerful storytelling technique. By painting a picture with words, storytellers can create a rich and immersive experience for the audience. Descriptive language can evoke emotions and stimulate the imagination, making the story more engaging and memorable. Sensory details, such as sights, sounds, smells, and textures, can transport the audience into the narrative, allowing them to experience the story on a visceral level. This sensory engagement enhances the emotional impact of the story, making it more resonant and meaningful.

Metaphors and symbolism are also effective tools in storytelling. They allow communicators to convey complex ideas and themes in a more accessible and relatable way. Metaphors create connections between seemingly unrelated concepts, offering new perspectives and insights. Symbolism adds depth and layers to the narrative, inviting the audience to interpret and reflect on the meaning behind the story. By using metaphors and symbolism, storytellers can create a richer and more nuanced narrative, enhancing the overall impact of the message.

Storytelling is not limited to verbal or written communication; it can also be expressed through visual and multimedia formats. Visual storytelling, such as films, photographs, and illustrations, can convey powerful messages without the need for words. These visual narratives can evoke emotions and tell stories in a way that transcends language barriers, making them accessible to a diverse audience. Multimedia storytelling, which combines text, images, audio, and video, offers a dynamic and interactive experience, engaging the audience on multiple levels.

The power of storytelling extends beyond individual communication; it can also be a powerful tool for organizations and brands. In the business world, storytelling is used to build brand identity, connect with customers, and communicate values and mission. By crafting a compelling brand story, organizations can differentiate themselves from competitors and create a loyal customer base. A strong brand story resonates with the audience, creating an emotional connection that fosters trust and loyalty.

In educational settings, storytelling can be a valuable pedagogical tool. It can make complex concepts more relatable and understandable, engaging students and enhancing learning outcomes. By incorporating storytelling into lessons, educators can create a more interactive and dynamic learning environment, encouraging students to think critically and creatively. Stories can also foster empathy and cultural understanding, as they expose students to diverse perspectives and experiences.

To harness the power of storytelling in communication, individuals can adopt several practical strategies. First, it is important to identify the core message or theme of the story. This provides direction and focus, ensuring that the narrative is coherent and purposeful. Next, consider the audience and tailor the story to their interests, needs, and preferences. Understanding the audience's perspective can inform the choice of characters, conflict, and language, making the story more relatable and engaging.

Practice is key to developing storytelling skills. By experimenting with different narrative techniques and styles, individuals can refine their ability to craft compelling stories. Seeking feedback from others can provide valuable insights into the effectiveness

of the story and areas for improvement.
Additionally, studying the work of skilled
storytellers, such as authors, filmmakers, and
speakers, can offer inspiration and guidance.

Adapting Your Message to Different Audiences

Understanding the nuances of communication is
essential for effectively conveying a message to
diverse audiences. Each audience comes with its own
set of expectations, cultural backgrounds, and levels
of understanding, making it crucial to tailor your
message accordingly. The art of adapting your
message involves recognizing these differences and
adjusting your communication style to ensure clarity,
engagement, and impact.

The first step in adapting your message is to identify
your audience. This involves analyzing the
demographic and psychographic characteristics of
the group you are addressing. Consider factors such
as age, gender, education level, cultural background,
and professional experience. Understanding these
elements will help you gauge the audience's prior
knowledge and expectations, allowing you to craft a
message that resonates with them.

Once you have a clear understanding of your audience, it's important to consider the context in which your message will be delivered. The setting, medium, and timing can all influence how your message is received. For instance, a formal presentation may require a different approach than a casual conversation. Similarly, delivering a message through written communication may necessitate a different tone and structure than a verbal presentation. By considering the context, you can ensure that your message is appropriate and effective.

Language plays a crucial role in adapting your message. The choice of words, tone, and style should align with the audience's preferences and level of understanding. For a technical audience, using industry-specific jargon and terminology may be appropriate, while a lay audience may require simpler language and explanations. It's important to strike a balance between being informative and accessible, ensuring that your message is both accurate and comprehensible.

Cultural sensitivity is another important aspect of adapting your message. Different cultures have varying communication norms and values, which can affect how your message is perceived. Being aware of cultural differences and showing respect for diverse perspectives can enhance your credibility and foster a positive connection with your audience. This may involve adjusting your language, tone, and even body language to align with cultural expectations.

Engaging your audience is key to ensuring that your message is received and understood. This involves capturing their attention and maintaining their interest throughout the communication process. Storytelling, humor, and relatable examples can be effective tools for engaging an audience, making your message more memorable and impactful. Additionally, encouraging interaction and feedback can create a more dynamic and participatory communication experience.

Feedback is an invaluable component of adapting your message. It provides insights into how your message is being received and allows you to make adjustments as needed. By actively seeking feedback from your audience, you can identify areas for improvement and refine your communication approach. This iterative process helps ensure that your message is clear, relevant, and effective.

Nonverbal communication is another important consideration when adapting your message. Body language, facial expressions, and gestures can all convey meaning and influence how your message is perceived. Being mindful of your nonverbal cues and ensuring they align with your verbal message can enhance your communication effectiveness.

Additionally, being attentive to the audience's nonverbal responses can provide valuable feedback on how your message is being received.

Adapting your message also involves being flexible and open to change. As you interact with different audiences, you may encounter unexpected challenges or opportunities that require you to adjust your approach. Being adaptable and responsive to the needs of your audience can enhance your credibility and effectiveness as a communicator.

Incorporating storytelling techniques can further enhance your ability to adapt your message. Stories have the power to engage, inspire, and persuade, making them a valuable tool in communication. By crafting a narrative that resonates with your audience, you can create an emotional connection and make your message more relatable and memorable. Consider using anecdotes, case studies, or personal experiences to illustrate key points and bring your message to life.

Empathy is a fundamental aspect of adapting your message. By putting yourself in the shoes of your audience, you can better understand their needs, concerns, and perspectives. This empathetic approach allows you to tailor your message in a way that resonates with the audience, fostering a sense of connection and understanding. Empathy also involves being attentive to the audience's reactions and adjusting your message accordingly to address any concerns or questions.

The medium through which you deliver your message can also impact its effectiveness. Different audiences may have preferences for certain communication channels, such as email, social media, or face-to-face interactions. By selecting the appropriate medium, you can ensure that your message reaches the audience in a way that is convenient and accessible for them. Additionally, considering the strengths and limitations of each medium can help you tailor your message to maximize its impact.

Adapting your message is not a one-size-fits-all approach; it requires continuous learning and refinement. As you gain experience and receive feedback, you can develop a deeper understanding of different audiences and how to effectively communicate with them. This ongoing process of adaptation and improvement is essential for becoming a skilled and effective communicator.

Avoiding Miscommunication and Misunderstandings

Miscommunication and misunderstandings are common pitfalls in the realm of human interaction, often leading to confusion, frustration, and even conflict. The ability to communicate effectively is a skill that can be honed with practice and awareness, and it is essential for fostering clear and meaningful exchanges. By understanding the root causes of miscommunication and implementing strategies to prevent them, individuals can enhance their interpersonal relationships and achieve more successful outcomes.

One of the primary causes of miscommunication is the assumption that others share the same knowledge, perspectives, and experiences. This assumption can lead to the use of ambiguous language or jargon that may not be understood by the listener. To avoid this, it is important to consider the listener's background and tailor your message accordingly. Providing context and clarifying terms can help bridge the gap between differing levels of understanding, ensuring that your message is received as intended.

Active listening is a crucial component in preventing misunderstandings. It involves fully engaging with the speaker, paying attention to both verbal and nonverbal cues, and providing feedback to confirm comprehension. By practicing active listening, individuals can demonstrate empathy and respect, creating an environment where open and honest communication can flourish. This approach not only reduces the likelihood of miscommunication but also strengthens the connection between the parties involved.

Nonverbal communication plays a significant role in conveying meaning and can often lead to misunderstandings if not aligned with verbal messages. Body language, facial expressions, and tone of voice can all influence how a message is perceived. Being mindful of these nonverbal cues and ensuring they are consistent with the spoken word can enhance clarity and prevent misinterpretations. Additionally, being aware of the listener's nonverbal responses can provide valuable insights into their level of understanding and engagement.

Cultural differences can also contribute to miscommunication, as different cultures have varying norms and expectations regarding communication styles. Being culturally sensitive and aware of these differences can help individuals navigate cross-cultural interactions more effectively. This may involve adjusting language, tone, and even gestures to align with cultural norms, demonstrating respect and consideration for diverse perspectives.

The choice of medium can impact the clarity of communication. Written communication, for example, lacks the immediate feedback and nonverbal cues present in face-to-face interactions, making it more susceptible to misinterpretation. To mitigate this, it is important to be clear and concise in written messages, using straightforward language and providing sufficient context. When possible, supplementing written communication with verbal interactions can help clarify any ambiguities and ensure mutual understanding.

Feedback is an essential tool for preventing and addressing misunderstandings. By actively seeking feedback from the listener, individuals can gauge the effectiveness of their communication and make necessary adjustments. This iterative process allows for continuous improvement and fosters a collaborative approach to communication. Encouraging open dialogue and creating a safe space for feedback can enhance trust and transparency, reducing the likelihood of miscommunication.

Emotional intelligence is another key factor in avoiding misunderstandings. It involves being aware of and managing one's own emotions, as well as recognizing and responding to the emotions of others. By cultivating emotional intelligence, individuals can navigate emotionally charged situations with greater ease, preventing misunderstandings that may arise from heightened emotions. This skill also enables individuals to communicate with empathy and compassion, fostering a deeper connection with others.

Clarification and confirmation are practical strategies for ensuring mutual understanding. When in doubt, asking questions to clarify the speaker's intent or repeating back what was heard can help confirm comprehension. This proactive approach not only prevents misunderstandings but also demonstrates a commitment to effective communication. By taking the time to clarify and confirm, individuals can avoid assumptions and ensure that their message is accurately received.

The use of storytelling can be an effective way to convey complex ideas and prevent misunderstandings. Stories have the power to engage and resonate with listeners, making abstract concepts more relatable and memorable. By incorporating storytelling techniques, individuals can illustrate key points and provide context, enhancing the clarity and impact of their message. This approach can also foster a sense of connection and shared understanding, reducing the potential for miscommunication.

Being mindful of language barriers is important in preventing misunderstandings, especially in diverse and multicultural settings. When communicating with individuals who may not be fluent in the same language, it is important to speak clearly and avoid idiomatic expressions or slang that may not be understood. Providing translations or using visual aids can also help bridge language gaps and ensure that the message is accessible to all parties involved.

Conflict resolution skills are valuable in addressing misunderstandings that may arise despite best efforts. By approaching conflicts with a problem-solving mindset and focusing on finding mutually beneficial solutions, individuals can resolve misunderstandings constructively. This involves active listening, empathy, and a willingness to compromise, fostering a collaborative and respectful approach to communication.

Incorporating humor can be a powerful tool in preventing and diffusing misunderstandings. Humor has the ability to lighten the mood and create a more relaxed atmosphere, making it easier to address potential miscommunications. However, it is important to use humor appropriately and be mindful of the audience's sensitivities, as humor can sometimes be misinterpreted or offend if not used with care.

Chapter 4

The Power of Nonverbal Communication

Understanding Body Language

Body language is a powerful form of nonverbal communication that can convey emotions, intentions, and attitudes without a single word being spoken. It encompasses a wide range of physical behaviors, including facial expressions, gestures, posture, and eye contact, all of which can significantly impact the way a message is perceived. Understanding body language is essential for effective communication, as it can provide valuable insights into the thoughts and feelings of others, as well as enhance one's ability to express themselves clearly and authentically.

Facial expressions are one of the most immediate and recognizable forms of body language. They can convey a wide array of emotions, from happiness and surprise to anger and sadness. The human face is capable of producing thousands of expressions, each with its own subtle nuances. For instance, a genuine smile, characterized by the crinkling of the eyes and the upward turning of the mouth, can convey warmth and friendliness, while a furrowed brow and pursed lips may indicate concern or disapproval. By paying attention to these cues, individuals can gain a deeper understanding of the emotional state of those around them and respond appropriately.

Gestures are another important aspect of body language, often used to emphasize or complement verbal communication. They can vary widely across cultures, with certain gestures holding different meanings in different contexts. For example, a thumbs-up gesture may be interpreted as a sign of approval in some cultures, while in others, it may be considered offensive. Understanding the cultural context of gestures is crucial for avoiding misunderstandings and ensuring that the intended message is conveyed accurately. Additionally, gestures can be used to express enthusiasm or engagement, such as nodding in agreement or using hand movements to illustrate a point.

Posture is a key indicator of confidence and openness. An upright posture with shoulders back and head held high can convey self-assurance and attentiveness, while slouching or crossing arms may suggest defensiveness or disinterest. Being mindful of one's posture can enhance the effectiveness of communication by projecting a positive and approachable demeanor. Similarly, observing the posture of others can provide insights into their level of comfort and engagement in a conversation.

Eye contact is a fundamental component of body language that can convey trust, interest, and sincerity. Maintaining appropriate eye contact can create a sense of connection and rapport, while avoiding eye contact may be perceived as evasive or disingenuous. However, the norms surrounding eye contact can vary across cultures, with some cultures considering direct eye contact as a sign of respect, while others may view it as confrontational. Being aware of these cultural differences can help individuals navigate social interactions more effectively and avoid potential misunderstandings.

Proxemics, or the study of personal space, is another important aspect of body language. The distance individuals maintain between themselves and others can convey a range of messages, from intimacy and affection to discomfort and aggression. Personal space preferences can vary based on cultural norms, individual personality, and the nature of the relationship. Being attuned to these preferences can help individuals gauge the appropriate level of physical proximity in different social situations, fostering a sense of comfort and respect.

Mirroring is a subtle yet powerful form of body language that involves unconsciously mimicking the gestures, posture, or expressions of another person.

This behavior can create a sense of rapport and empathy, as it signals that individuals are in sync with one another. By being aware of mirroring, individuals can consciously use it to build connections and enhance communication. However, it is important to use mirroring judiciously, as excessive or forced mirroring may come across as insincere or manipulative.

The tone and pace of voice, while not strictly part of body language, are closely related and can significantly influence the interpretation of a message. A calm and steady tone can convey confidence and authority, while a hurried or high-pitched tone may suggest anxiety or uncertainty. Similarly, varying the pace of speech can emphasize key points and maintain the listener's interest. Being mindful of these vocal cues can enhance the clarity and impact of communication, complementing the nonverbal signals conveyed through body language.

Understanding body language also involves recognizing the potential for misinterpretation. Nonverbal cues can be ambiguous and open to multiple interpretations, depending on the context and the individual's personal biases. For example, a person crossing their arms may be perceived as defensive, but they may simply be feeling cold or comfortable in that position. To avoid misinterpretation, it is important to consider the broader context and look for clusters of nonverbal cues that reinforce a particular message.

Developing an awareness of one's own body language can enhance self-expression and communication effectiveness. By being conscious of the signals being sent through facial expressions, gestures, and posture, individuals can ensure that their nonverbal communication aligns with their verbal message. This alignment creates a sense of authenticity and credibility, fostering trust and understanding in interpersonal interactions.

Practicing mindfulness and observation can improve one's ability to read and interpret body language. By paying attention to the nonverbal cues of others and reflecting on their own body language, individuals can develop a heightened awareness of the subtleties of communication. This practice can lead to more meaningful and effective interactions, as individuals become more attuned to the emotions and intentions of those around them.

The Role of Facial Expressions and Eye Contact

Facial expressions and eye contact are integral components of human communication, serving as windows into the emotions and intentions of individuals. These nonverbal cues can convey a wealth of information, often more powerfully than words alone. Understanding the role of facial expressions and eye contact can enhance interpersonal interactions, allowing for more authentic and effective communication.

Facial expressions are among the most universal forms of nonverbal communication, transcending language barriers and cultural differences. The human face is capable of producing a vast array of expressions, each capable of conveying complex emotions and subtle nuances. From the joy reflected in a beaming smile to the sorrow etched in a furrowed brow, facial expressions provide a direct insight into a person's emotional state. They can reveal feelings of happiness, surprise, anger, fear, disgust, and sadness, often without the need for verbal articulation.

The universality of facial expressions is rooted in their evolutionary significance. As social creatures, humans have developed the ability to quickly interpret facial cues as a means of survival. Recognizing a threat or understanding the intentions of others through their expressions has historically been crucial for navigating social environments. This innate ability to read faces continues to play a vital role in modern communication, influencing how individuals perceive and respond to one another.

Eye contact, another critical aspect of nonverbal communication, serves as a powerful tool for establishing connection and conveying sincerity. The eyes are often referred to as the "windows to the soul," and for good reason. They can express a range of emotions, from warmth and affection to suspicion and hostility. Maintaining eye contact can signal attentiveness and interest, fostering a sense of trust and rapport between individuals. Conversely, avoiding eye contact may be perceived as evasive or disingenuous, potentially undermining the credibility of the speaker.

The cultural context of eye contact is important to consider, as norms and expectations can vary widely across different societies. In some cultures, direct eye contact is seen as a sign of respect and engagement, while in others, it may be considered confrontational or disrespectful. Understanding these cultural nuances is essential for navigating cross-cultural interactions and ensuring that the intended message is conveyed accurately.

Facial expressions and eye contact work in tandem to enhance communication, providing a rich tapestry of nonverbal cues that complement verbal messages. For example, a smile accompanied by warm eye contact can reinforce a friendly greeting, while a stern expression paired with a piercing gaze can underscore a serious warning. By aligning facial expressions and eye contact with verbal communication, individuals can create a more cohesive and impactful message.

The ability to interpret facial expressions and eye contact is not only valuable in personal interactions but also in professional settings. In negotiations, for instance, being attuned to the nonverbal cues of others can provide insights into their level of interest, agreement, or resistance. Similarly, in leadership roles, effectively using facial expressions and eye contact can inspire confidence and motivate teams, fostering a positive and productive work environment.

Developing an awareness of one's own facial expressions and eye contact can enhance self-expression and communication effectiveness. By being mindful of the signals being sent through these nonverbal cues, individuals can ensure that their expressions align with their verbal message, creating a sense of authenticity and credibility. This alignment is particularly important in situations where emotions may be heightened, such as during conflicts or negotiations, as it can help to de-escalate tensions and facilitate constructive dialogue.

Practicing mindfulness and observation can improve one's ability to read and interpret facial expressions and eye contact. By paying attention to the nonverbal cues of others and reflecting on their own expressions, individuals can develop a heightened awareness of the subtleties of communication. This practice can lead to more meaningful and effective interactions, as individuals become more attuned to the emotions and intentions of those around them.

Using Gestures to Enhance Your Message

Gestures are a fundamental aspect of human communication, serving as a dynamic extension of verbal language. They can amplify, clarify, and even substitute spoken words, making them an invaluable tool for enhancing messages. Understanding how to effectively use gestures can significantly improve communication skills, allowing individuals to convey their thoughts and emotions with greater precision and impact.

The use of gestures is deeply rooted in human evolution, with evidence suggesting that they predate spoken language. As a form of nonverbal communication, gestures can transcend linguistic barriers, enabling people from different cultures and backgrounds to understand each other. This universality makes gestures a powerful means of expression, capable of conveying complex ideas and emotions without the need for words.

There are various types of gestures, each serving a distinct purpose in communication. Emblems are gestures with specific, culturally understood meanings, such as a thumbs-up for approval or a wave for greeting. Illustrators accompany speech, adding emphasis or clarity to the spoken message. For example, a person might use hand movements to describe the size or shape of an object. Regulators help manage the flow of conversation, signaling when it's someone else's turn to speak or when a speaker is about to conclude. Adaptors are often unconscious gestures that reveal a person's emotional state, such as fidgeting when nervous or tapping a foot when impatient.

The effectiveness of gestures in communication lies in their ability to engage multiple senses, creating a more immersive experience for the audience. By incorporating gestures into speech, speakers can capture attention, maintain interest, and facilitate understanding. This multisensory approach can be particularly beneficial in educational settings, where complex concepts may be more easily grasped through visual demonstration.

To harness the power of gestures, it's essential to be mindful of their cultural context. While some gestures may be universally recognized, others can have different meanings in different cultures. For instance, the "OK" hand gesture is a positive sign in some countries but considered offensive in others. Being aware of these cultural nuances can prevent misunderstandings and ensure that the intended message is conveyed accurately.

Incorporating gestures into communication requires a balance between natural expression and intentionality. Overly exaggerated or forced gestures can appear insincere or distracting, while subtle, purposeful gestures can enhance the message and reinforce the speaker's credibility. Practicing in front of a mirror or recording oneself can help individuals become more aware of their gestures and refine their delivery.

Gestures can also play a crucial role in building rapport and establishing connection with an audience. By mirroring the gestures of others, individuals can create a sense of empathy and understanding, fostering a more collaborative and harmonious interaction. This technique, known as "gestural synchrony," can be particularly effective in negotiations or conflict resolution, where establishing common ground is essential.

In professional settings, the strategic use of gestures can enhance presentations and public speaking engagements. A well-timed gesture can underscore a key point, making it more memorable for the audience. For example, a speaker might use an open palm gesture to convey honesty and transparency or a pointing gesture to direct attention to a specific visual aid. By aligning gestures with the content of the presentation, speakers can create a more cohesive and impactful message.

The role of gestures in communication extends beyond face-to-face interactions, influencing how messages are perceived in digital and virtual environments. In video calls or online presentations, gestures can help compensate for the lack of physical presence, adding a layer of expressiveness that enhances engagement. Being mindful of camera angles and framing can ensure that gestures are visible and effective in these settings.

Developing an awareness of one's own gestures and their impact on communication can lead to more effective and authentic interactions. By observing the gestures of others and reflecting on their own, individuals can gain insights into the subtleties of nonverbal communication and refine their skills. This practice can lead to more meaningful connections and a deeper understanding of the emotions and intentions of those around them.

The Influence of Posture and Space

Posture and space are two critical elements in the realm of nonverbal communication, often speaking volumes before a single word is uttered. The way individuals carry themselves and the space they occupy can convey confidence, authority, openness, or defensiveness. Understanding the influence of posture and space can significantly enhance one's ability to communicate effectively and interpret the unspoken messages of others.

Posture, the alignment and positioning of the body, is a powerful indicator of a person's emotional state and attitude. An upright posture, with shoulders back and head held high, often signals confidence and self-assurance. It projects an image of competence and readiness, making it an essential aspect of professional and social interactions. Conversely, slouched shoulders and a downward gaze can suggest insecurity or disinterest, potentially undermining the speaker's credibility and engagement with the audience.

The impact of posture extends beyond personal perception, influencing how others respond and interact. In a business meeting, for example, a leader who maintains an open and assertive posture is more likely to command respect and attention from colleagues. This nonverbal cue can set the tone for the entire interaction, fostering an environment of trust and collaboration. Similarly, in social settings, individuals who exhibit positive posture are often perceived as more approachable and friendly, facilitating smoother and more meaningful connections.

Space, or proxemics, refers to the physical distance maintained between individuals during communication. This spatial arrangement can vary significantly across cultures and contexts, influencing the dynamics of interaction. In Western cultures, for instance, maintaining a certain level of personal space is customary, with closer proximity reserved for intimate or familiar relationships. In contrast, other cultures may embrace closer distances as a sign of warmth and engagement.

The concept of personal space is deeply ingrained in human psychology, serving as a protective boundary that individuals instinctively maintain. Invading this space can trigger discomfort or anxiety, potentially hindering effective communication. Being mindful of spatial boundaries is crucial, particularly in diverse or multicultural environments where norms may differ. By respecting these boundaries, individuals can create a sense of safety and respect, fostering more open and productive exchanges.

The strategic use of space can also convey power dynamics and influence perceptions. In a professional setting, occupying a larger physical space, such as a spacious office or a prominent position at a conference table, can signal authority and status. This spatial arrangement can subtly reinforce hierarchical structures, impacting how messages are received and interpreted. Conversely, choosing to share space or reduce physical barriers can promote inclusivity and collaboration, breaking down perceived power imbalances.

Posture and space are not static elements but can be adapted to suit different contexts and objectives. In public speaking, for instance, a speaker may use expansive gestures and movement to engage a large audience, while maintaining a grounded posture to convey stability and confidence. Similarly, in a one-on-one conversation, leaning slightly forward and reducing physical distance can demonstrate attentiveness and empathy, strengthening the connection with the listener.

Awareness of posture and space can also enhance one's ability to read and respond to the nonverbal cues of others. By observing shifts in posture or changes in spatial dynamics, individuals can gain insights into the emotions and intentions of those around them. This heightened sensitivity can inform more effective communication strategies, allowing for timely adjustments in tone, content, or delivery.

Developing an understanding of posture and space requires practice and self-awareness. Individuals can benefit from reflecting on their own nonverbal habits and experimenting with different postures and spatial arrangements. Seeking feedback from trusted peers or mentors can provide valuable insights into how one's nonverbal communication is perceived and where improvements can be made.

Interpreting Nonverbal Cues from Others

Nonverbal cues are the silent language of human interaction, often revealing more than spoken words. These cues encompass a wide range of behaviors, including facial expressions, gestures, posture, eye contact, and even the tone of voice. Understanding and interpreting these signals can provide valuable insights into the emotions, intentions, and attitudes of others, enhancing communication and fostering deeper connections.

Facial expressions are among the most universal and easily recognizable nonverbal cues. The human face is capable of conveying a vast array of emotions, from joy and surprise to anger and sadness. A smile can indicate friendliness and openness, while a furrowed brow may suggest confusion or concern. By paying attention to these subtle changes, one can gauge the emotional state of others and respond appropriately. However, it's important to consider the context and cultural differences, as expressions may vary in meaning across different societies.

Gestures, the movements of the hands and arms, also play a significant role in nonverbal communication. They can emphasize or complement verbal messages, adding depth and clarity to the spoken word. For instance, a thumbs-up gesture is widely recognized as a sign of approval or agreement, while crossed arms might indicate defensiveness or resistance. Observing these gestures can provide clues about a person's level of engagement or agreement with the conversation. Yet, it's crucial to be mindful of cultural variations, as gestures can hold different meanings in different parts of the world.

Posture, the way individuals hold their bodies, can reveal much about their confidence and attitude. An open posture, with arms relaxed and body facing the speaker, suggests attentiveness and receptivity. In contrast, a closed posture, such as crossed arms or legs, may indicate discomfort or disagreement. By observing these cues, one can adjust their approach to foster a more positive and productive interaction.

Additionally, mirroring the posture of others can create a sense of rapport and mutual understanding, enhancing the overall communication experience.

Eye contact is a powerful nonverbal cue that can convey trust, interest, and sincerity. Maintaining appropriate eye contact demonstrates attentiveness and respect, signaling that one is fully engaged in the conversation. However, excessive or prolonged eye contact can be perceived as intrusive or aggressive, while avoiding eye contact may suggest disinterest or evasiveness. Striking the right balance is key, and being attuned to the cultural norms and individual preferences of others can help navigate this delicate aspect of communication.

The tone of voice, though often considered a verbal element, carries significant nonverbal weight. Variations in pitch, volume, and pace can convey emotions and attitudes that words alone may not fully capture. A warm and steady tone can express confidence and empathy, while a high-pitched or hurried tone might indicate anxiety or urgency. By listening carefully to these vocal cues, one can gain a deeper understanding of the speaker's emotional state and adjust their response accordingly.

Interpreting nonverbal cues requires a keen sense of observation and an open mind. It's essential to consider the entire context of the interaction, including the environment, cultural background, and individual differences. Nonverbal signals are often complex and multifaceted, and relying on a single cue can lead to misunderstandings. Instead, look for clusters of cues that align with the verbal message and the overall situation.

Developing the ability to read nonverbal cues can enhance personal and professional relationships. In a business setting, for example, understanding the unspoken signals of colleagues or clients can inform negotiation strategies and decision-making processes. In social interactions, being attuned to the emotions and needs of others can foster empathy and strengthen bonds.

Practicing active listening and observation can improve one's ability to interpret nonverbal cues. This involves giving full attention to the speaker, observing their body language, and reflecting on the emotions and intentions behind their words. Seeking feedback from others and engaging in self-reflection can also provide valuable insights into one's own nonverbal communication style and areas for improvement.

Chapter 5

Mastering Emotional Intelligence in Communication

Recognizing and Managing Your Emotions

Emotions are the vibrant threads that weave the tapestry of human experience, influencing thoughts, actions, and interactions. Recognizing and managing these emotions is a crucial skill that can lead to personal growth, improved relationships, and enhanced well-being. The journey begins with self-awareness, the ability to identify and understand one's own emotions as they arise.

Self-awareness involves tuning into the subtle signals that emotions send, such as physical sensations, thoughts, and behavioral impulses. For instance, anger might manifest as a tightening of the jaw or a racing heartbeat, while sadness could feel like a heaviness in the chest. By paying attention to these cues, individuals can begin to label their emotions accurately, distinguishing between similar feelings like frustration and disappointment. This process of naming emotions is a powerful step toward gaining control over them.

Once emotions are recognized, the next step is to understand their origins and triggers. Emotions often arise in response to specific events, thoughts, or memories. By reflecting on the circumstances that lead to certain emotional responses, individuals can uncover patterns and identify recurring triggers. This insight allows for a deeper understanding of the underlying needs and desires that drive emotional reactions. For example, feeling anxious before a presentation might stem from a desire for approval or fear of failure. Recognizing these root causes can empower individuals to address them more effectively.

Managing emotions involves regulating their intensity and expression in a healthy and constructive manner. One effective strategy is cognitive reappraisal, which involves reframing a situation to alter its emotional impact. For instance, viewing a challenging task as an opportunity for growth rather than a threat can reduce feelings of anxiety and increase motivation. This shift in perspective can be achieved through positive self-talk, focusing on strengths and past successes, and visualizing positive outcomes.

Another valuable technique for managing emotions is mindfulness, the practice of staying present and fully engaged in the current moment. Mindfulness encourages individuals to observe their emotions without judgment, allowing them to pass naturally without being overwhelmed. Techniques such as deep breathing, meditation, and grounding exercises can help cultivate mindfulness and create a sense of calm and clarity. By practicing mindfulness regularly, individuals can develop greater emotional resilience and reduce the impact of stressors.

Expressing emotions in a healthy way is also essential for emotional management. Bottling up emotions can lead to increased stress and negative health outcomes, while unchecked emotional outbursts can damage relationships and reputations. Finding appropriate outlets for emotional expression, such as talking to a trusted friend, journaling, or engaging in creative activities, can provide relief and insight. Additionally, assertive communication skills can help individuals express their emotions and needs clearly and respectfully, fostering understanding and connection with others.

Emotional intelligence, the ability to recognize, understand, and manage emotions in oneself and others, plays a significant role in effective emotion management. Developing emotional intelligence involves honing skills such as empathy, active listening, and conflict resolution. Empathy allows individuals to connect with others' emotions and perspectives, fostering compassion and reducing misunderstandings. Active listening involves fully engaging with others' words and emotions, creating a supportive environment for open communication. Conflict resolution skills enable individuals to navigate disagreements and find mutually beneficial solutions, reducing emotional tension and promoting harmony.

Building a strong support network can also enhance emotional management. Surrounding oneself with supportive and understanding individuals provides a safe space for emotional expression and growth. Trusted friends, family members, or mental health professionals can offer guidance, encouragement, and perspective during challenging times. Engaging in social activities and community involvement can also provide a sense of belonging and purpose, boosting emotional well-being.

Self-care practices are integral to maintaining emotional balance and resilience. Prioritizing physical health through regular exercise, a balanced diet, and adequate sleep can positively impact emotional regulation. Engaging in activities that bring joy and relaxation, such as hobbies, nature walks, or spending time with loved ones, can replenish emotional reserves and reduce stress. Setting boundaries and managing time effectively can prevent burnout and create space for self-reflection and rejuvenation.

Understanding the Emotions of Others

Empathy is the bridge that connects us to the emotions of others, allowing us to step into their shoes and perceive the world from their perspective. Understanding the emotions of others is a skill that enriches relationships, fosters compassion, and enhances communication. It begins with active listening, a practice that involves fully engaging with the speaker, not just hearing their words but also observing their non-verbal cues. Facial expressions, body language, and tone of voice often convey more than words alone. A furrowed brow might indicate confusion or concern, while a gentle smile can signal warmth and openness. By paying attention to these subtle signals, we can gain a deeper understanding of the emotions being expressed.

Cultivating empathy requires an open mind and a willingness to suspend judgment. It's about setting aside preconceived notions and allowing oneself to be present with another's experience. This openness creates a safe space for others to share their feelings honestly and vulnerably. When someone feels truly heard and understood, it can be a powerful and healing experience. Empathy is not about solving problems or offering advice; it's about being there, offering support, and acknowledging the emotions of others.

Perspective-taking is another essential component of understanding others' emotions. It involves imagining oneself in another person's situation and considering how they might feel. This mental exercise can reveal insights into their emotional state and motivations. For example, a colleague who seems irritable might be dealing with stress at home, or a friend who withdraws might be experiencing feelings of inadequacy. By considering these possibilities, we can respond with greater sensitivity and compassion.

Emotional intelligence plays a significant role in understanding others' emotions. It involves recognizing and interpreting emotional cues, both verbal and non-verbal, and responding appropriately. Developing emotional intelligence requires self-awareness, as understanding our own emotions can help us relate to the emotions of others. It also involves empathy, social skills, and the ability to manage relationships effectively. By honing these skills, we can navigate social interactions with greater ease and build stronger connections.

Communication is a vital tool for understanding emotions. Asking open-ended questions encourages others to share their feelings and experiences. Questions like "How did that make you feel?" or "What was going through your mind?" invite deeper exploration and expression. Reflective listening, where we paraphrase what the other person has said, can also demonstrate understanding and validate their emotions. This technique shows that we are engaged and interested in their perspective.

Cultural awareness is an important aspect of understanding emotions, as cultural backgrounds can influence how emotions are expressed and perceived. Different cultures have varying norms and expectations regarding emotional expression. For instance, some cultures may value emotional restraint, while others encourage open expression. Being mindful of these differences can prevent misunderstandings and foster more inclusive and respectful interactions. It requires a willingness to learn and adapt, recognizing that there is no one-size-fits-all approach to emotional expression.

Building trust is essential for understanding emotions, as people are more likely to share their true feelings when they feel safe and supported. Trust is built through consistency, reliability, and authenticity. By being genuine and transparent in our interactions, we create an environment where others feel comfortable opening up. Trust also involves respecting boundaries and confidentiality, ensuring that shared emotions are treated with care and discretion.

Understanding the emotions of others can be challenging, especially when faced with strong or conflicting emotions. It's important to remain patient and compassionate, recognizing that emotions are complex and multifaceted. Sometimes, people may not fully understand their own emotions, and it may take time for them to articulate their feelings. Offering a listening ear and a supportive presence can make a significant difference, even when words are hard to find.

Practicing self-care is crucial when engaging with others' emotions, as it can be emotionally taxing. Setting boundaries and taking time for oneself can prevent burnout and ensure that we have the emotional capacity to support others. Engaging in activities that replenish our energy and bring joy can help maintain emotional balance and resilience.

Building Emotional Connections Through Communication

Communication is the lifeline of human connection, a dynamic dance of words, gestures, and expressions that weaves the fabric of relationships. Building emotional connections through communication involves more than just exchanging information; it requires a genuine engagement with the thoughts and feelings of others. At its core, effective communication is about creating a shared understanding, a meeting of minds and hearts that transcends mere words.

The foundation of emotional connection through communication lies in active listening. This involves more than just hearing the words spoken; it requires an attentive presence, an openness to the nuances of tone, pace, and body language. When we listen actively, we signal to the other person that their words matter, that their emotions are valid and worthy of attention. This validation fosters trust and encourages deeper sharing, laying the groundwork for a meaningful connection.

Empathy is the bridge that connects us to the emotional world of others. It involves stepping into their shoes, seeing the world through their eyes, and feeling with their hearts. Empathetic communication is about acknowledging and validating emotions, even when they differ from our own. It's about saying, "I see you, I hear you, and I understand." This empathetic stance creates a safe space for vulnerability, where individuals feel comfortable expressing their true selves without fear of judgment or rejection.

Non-verbal communication plays a crucial role in building emotional connections. Our facial expressions, gestures, and posture often convey more than words alone. A warm smile, a reassuring nod, or a gentle touch can communicate understanding and support in ways that words cannot. Being mindful of these non-verbal cues enhances our ability to connect emotionally, as it demonstrates attentiveness and care.

The art of asking open-ended questions is a powerful tool in fostering emotional connections. These questions invite exploration and reflection, encouraging others to share their thoughts and feelings more deeply. Instead of seeking specific answers, open-ended questions create a dialogue, a back-and-forth exchange that enriches understanding. Questions like "What was that experience like for you?" or "How did you feel about that?" open the door to meaningful conversations that strengthen emotional bonds.

Authenticity is the cornerstone of genuine communication. When we communicate authentically, we present our true selves, free from pretense or facade. This honesty invites reciprocity, encouraging others to be authentic in return. Authentic communication builds trust, as it assures others that we are reliable and sincere. It also fosters a sense of belonging, as individuals feel accepted for who they truly are.

Emotional intelligence is a key component in building emotional connections through communication. It involves recognizing and managing our own emotions, as well as understanding and influencing the emotions of others. By developing emotional intelligence, we enhance our ability to navigate complex social interactions, respond to emotional cues, and build rapport. This skill allows us to communicate with empathy and sensitivity, fostering deeper connections.

Conflict is an inevitable part of human interaction, but it can also be an opportunity for growth and connection. Constructive communication during conflict involves expressing emotions honestly and respectfully, while also being open to the perspectives of others. It's about finding common ground and working collaboratively towards a resolution. By approaching conflict with a mindset of understanding and cooperation, we can strengthen emotional connections and build resilience in relationships.

Cultural awareness is an important aspect of communication, as cultural backgrounds can influence how emotions are expressed and interpreted. Being mindful of cultural differences enhances our ability to connect with individuals from diverse backgrounds. It requires a willingness to learn and adapt, recognizing that there are multiple ways of expressing and understanding emotions. This cultural sensitivity fosters inclusivity and respect, enriching our communication and connections.

The Role of Empathy in Effective Communication

Empathy is the silent force that breathes life into communication, transforming mere exchanges of words into profound connections. It is the ability to understand and share the feelings of another, a skill that transcends the boundaries of language and culture. In the realm of effective communication, empathy serves as a bridge, linking individuals through shared emotional experiences and fostering a sense of belonging and understanding.

At the heart of empathetic communication lies the capacity to listen deeply. This involves more than just hearing the words spoken; it requires an attunement to the emotional undertones and unspoken messages that accompany them. When we listen with empathy, we create a space where others feel valued and understood, encouraging them to open up and share more authentically. This deep listening is a powerful tool for building trust and rapport, as it demonstrates a genuine interest in the other person's perspective and emotions.

Empathy also involves recognizing and validating the emotions of others. This means acknowledging their feelings without judgment or dismissal, even when those feelings differ from our own. By validating emotions, we communicate that we respect and accept the other person's experience, which can be incredibly affirming and comforting. This validation fosters a sense of safety and openness, allowing for more honest and meaningful exchanges.

The role of empathy in effective communication extends to the ability to express our own emotions in a way that is considerate of others. This involves being mindful of how our words and actions may impact those around us, and striving to communicate in a way that is respectful and compassionate. By expressing ourselves with empathy, we create an environment where others feel comfortable doing the same, leading to more authentic and productive interactions.

Empathy also plays a crucial role in conflict resolution. When disagreements arise, it can be easy to become entrenched in our own viewpoints, dismissing the perspectives of others. However, by approaching conflict with empathy, we can better understand the underlying emotions and motivations driving the other person's behavior. This understanding allows us to address the root causes of the conflict, rather than just the surface-level issues, leading to more effective and lasting resolutions.

In addition to its role in conflict resolution, empathy enhances collaboration and teamwork. In group settings, empathetic communication fosters a sense of unity and cooperation, as individuals feel valued and understood. This sense of belonging encourages open dialogue and the sharing of diverse perspectives, leading to more innovative and effective solutions. By cultivating empathy within teams, we create an environment where everyone feels empowered to contribute and collaborate.

Empathy is not an innate trait, but a skill that can be developed and strengthened over time. One way to cultivate empathy is through active listening, which involves giving our full attention to the speaker and seeking to understand their perspective without interruption or judgment. This practice helps us to become more attuned to the emotions and needs of others, enhancing our ability to communicate empathetically.

Another way to develop empathy is through perspective-taking, which involves imagining ourselves in the other person's situation and considering how we might feel in their shoes. This exercise helps us to better understand and relate to the emotions and experiences of others, fostering a deeper sense of connection and understanding.

Empathy can also be cultivated through mindfulness, which involves being present and fully engaged in the moment. By practicing mindfulness, we become more aware of our own emotions and reactions, as well as those of others. This heightened awareness allows us to respond to others with greater sensitivity and compassion, enhancing our ability to communicate empathetically.

The benefits of empathetic communication extend beyond individual interactions, impacting the broader social and cultural landscape. In a world that is increasingly interconnected, empathy serves as a vital tool for bridging cultural divides and fostering mutual understanding. By approaching communication with empathy, we can break down barriers and build bridges of connection, creating a more inclusive and harmonious society.

Strategies for Emotional Regulation

Emotional regulation is an essential skill that allows individuals to manage and respond to their emotions in a healthy and constructive manner. It involves the ability to recognize, understand, and modulate one's emotional responses, ensuring that emotions do not overwhelm or dictate behavior. Developing effective strategies for emotional regulation can lead to improved mental health, better relationships, and enhanced overall well-being.

One fundamental strategy for emotional regulation is self-awareness. This involves cultivating an understanding of one's emotional triggers and patterns. By identifying the situations, people, or thoughts that provoke strong emotional reactions, individuals can begin to anticipate and prepare for these responses. Self-awareness also includes recognizing the physical sensations and thoughts that accompany different emotions, allowing for a more comprehensive understanding of one's emotional landscape.

Mindfulness is another powerful tool for emotional regulation. This practice involves paying attention to the present moment without judgment, allowing individuals to observe their emotions as they arise without becoming entangled in them. Mindfulness encourages a non-reactive stance towards emotions, fostering a sense of calm and clarity. By practicing mindfulness regularly, individuals can develop greater emotional resilience and the ability to respond to emotions with intention rather than impulsivity.

Cognitive reappraisal is a technique that involves changing the way one thinks about a situation in order to alter its emotional impact. This strategy requires individuals to challenge and reframe negative or distorted thoughts, replacing them with more balanced and constructive perspectives. For example, instead of viewing a setback as a personal failure, one might reframe it as an opportunity for growth and learning. Cognitive reappraisal can help individuals manage their emotions more effectively by reducing the intensity of negative emotional responses.

Another effective strategy for emotional regulation is the development of healthy coping mechanisms. These are activities or behaviors that help individuals manage stress and emotions in a constructive way. Examples of healthy coping mechanisms include exercise, creative expression, spending time in nature, and engaging in hobbies. By incorporating these activities into their daily routine, individuals can create a buffer against stress and enhance their emotional well-being.

Social support is also a crucial component of emotional regulation. Having a network of supportive friends, family, or peers provides individuals with a sense of connection and belonging, which can be incredibly grounding during times of emotional distress. Sharing emotions with trusted others can offer validation and perspective, helping individuals process and regulate their feelings more effectively. Building and maintaining strong social connections can serve as a protective factor against emotional dysregulation.

In addition to these strategies, it is important to develop effective communication skills. Expressing emotions in a clear and respectful manner can prevent misunderstandings and reduce emotional tension in relationships. This involves using "I" statements to convey feelings without blaming or criticizing others, as well as actively listening to the emotions and perspectives of others. By fostering open and empathetic communication, individuals can create an environment that supports emotional regulation.

Physical self-care is another essential aspect of emotional regulation. Ensuring that one's basic needs are met, such as getting enough sleep, eating a balanced diet, and engaging in regular physical activity, can have a significant impact on emotional well-being. When the body is well-nourished and rested, individuals are better equipped to manage their emotions and respond to stressors in a balanced way.

It is also important to recognize the role of emotional acceptance in regulation. This involves acknowledging and accepting emotions as they arise, without attempting to suppress or avoid them. Emotional acceptance allows individuals to experience their emotions fully, which can lead to greater insight and understanding. By accepting emotions, individuals can reduce the struggle against them and create space for more adaptive responses.

Developing a personal emotional regulation plan can be a helpful way to integrate these strategies into daily life. This plan might include identifying specific triggers, setting goals for emotional regulation, and outlining the strategies and coping mechanisms that work best for the individual. By having a clear plan in place, individuals can approach emotional regulation with intention and consistency.

Practicing gratitude is another strategy that can enhance emotional regulation. By focusing on the positive aspects of life and expressing appreciation for them, individuals can shift their attention away from negative emotions and cultivate a more positive outlook. Keeping a gratitude journal or regularly reflecting on things to be thankful for can help reinforce this mindset and contribute to emotional well-being.

Finally, seeking professional support can be an invaluable resource for emotional regulation.

Therapists and counselors can provide guidance and support in developing personalized strategies for managing emotions. They can also offer tools and techniques for addressing underlying issues that may contribute to emotional dysregulation. Engaging in therapy can be a proactive step towards achieving greater emotional balance and resilience.